To my d
with all

THE HEART OF
DEVON

Lionel Aggett

HALSGROVE

First published in Great Britain in 2003

Title page painting: *Winter's Coat, Southernhay*, Pastel, 150x150mm

British Library Cataloguing-in-Publication Data
A CIP record for this title is available from the British Library

ISBN 1 84114 290 5

HALSGROVE

Halsgrove House
Lower Moor Way
Tiverton, Devon EX16 6SS
Tel: 01884 243242
Fax: 01884 243325
email: sales@halsgrove.com
website: www.halsgrove.com

Printed and bound by D'Auria Industrie Grafiche Spa, Italy

CONTENTS

Stokeinteignhead to Dartmoor
Pastel, 250x325mm

ACKNOWLEDGEMENTS

I would like to thank David and Ian Walker for hosting the launch of this book during the solo exhibition 'The Heart of Devon' held at the Walker Galleries, Honiton, the sister gallery of their three galleries in Harrogate, where my work is also represented. My thanks also to the following owners of my work whose paintings and drawings have been reproduced here: Mr & Mrs R. Adams, Mr R.G. Aggett, Mr & Mrs R.J. Aggett, Miss N.A. Batro, Mrs J. Beament, Mr & Mrs A. Bowden, Mr & Mrs P. Bisson, Bradford & Bingley Building Society, Mr & Mrs Paul Brewer, Mr & Mrs Peter Brewer, Mr & Mrs P. Brown, Mr & Mrs M. Brown, Mr & Mrs I Campbell, Mr & Mrs N Cheffers (deceased), Mr & Mrs J. Clark, Miss P.A. Cowler, Cornwall County Council, Mr & Mrs K. Davison, Mr & Mrs C. De Verenne, Devonshire & Dorset Regiment Officers Mess, Downes Crediton Golf Club, Mr & Mrs P. Evans, Exeter City Council, Exeter Health Care, Mr & Mrs Friend, Mr & Mrs N. Gardner, Mr & Mrs M. Gibbs, Mr Stephen Gratton, Mrs M. Grisman, Mr & Mrs A.J. Hamilton, Mr & Mrs Harris, Mr & Mrs T. Hellawell, Mr & Mrs E. Holden, Mr Alan Humphries, Mr & Mrs J. Hunter, Dr C.D. Jefferiss, K.P.M.G. Peat Marwick, Mr & Mrs J. Laurence, Mr & Mrs C. Mann, Mr & Mrs Marchant, Mrs C.V. Nelson, Mr & Mrs N. Page, Mr & Mrs A. Parr, Mr & Mrs B. Reeves, Mrs S. Rising, Mr & Mrs N. Rising, Mr & Mrs P. Rose, Mr & Mrs C. Rowlands, Mr & Mrs A. Ruddock, Mr Martyn Smale, Mr & Mrs A. Smith, Beth Sims, Mr & Mrs Stephen Sims, Mr & Mrs G. Sturtridge, Mr & Mrs H. Tasker, Dr & Mrs G Wallen, Mrs S. Wagg, Mr & Mrs B. Webb, Mr & Mrs D. White, Mr & Mrs D. Whitworth, Mr & Mrs G. Wood, Mrs C. Wright, Mr Simon Young.

My appreciation to all patrons who supported me locally during the early days, and to those purchasers whose paintings, due to space restriction, are not featured here.

My sincere thanks to Stephen Sims whose excellent poems are quoted from the collections 'Kirtonsong' (Cervisian Press, Crediton) and 'Southern Hay' (word pictures accompanying an exhibition held at the Royal Clarence Hotel, Exeter).

All of the illustrated diary extracts (I also produce these working diaries when on my travels), are taken from my 2000 millennium diary.

The drawing 'The Devastation' (High Street) is based on an *Express & Echo* blitz photograph by a cameraman now unknown, illustrated in Geoff Worrall's *Target Exeter*.

Thanks once again to John Melville, photographer for producing the necessary transparencies; also to Jane Henderson of the Gilders Workshop, and my brother Reginald for framing the exhibition, 'The Heart of Devon'.

This book is dedicated to my wife Anne and our family. Also Dustin our tabby (Sennen is sadly no longer with us), to livestock and wildlife at large, and to all those who farm and tend this wonderful landscape of ours.

Jazz at the 'Jolly Porter', Exeter   Pastel, 250x325mm

FOREWORD

Lionel Aggett is an artist who has truly responded to the land-scape and colour of Devon. From the high moors of Dartmoor or Exmoor down to the City of Exeter, a lifetime of observation is contained within these covers. Whether painting his parents' areas of Drewsteignton and the Tamar Valley or his own familiar landscape near Crediton, he has a natural feeling for landscape and light. He captures with sensitivity the changing seasons, creating a balance and harmony from nature true to the very roots of the landscape. Here he records poetry of the red soil of Devon, the wide skies which evoke the stillness of summer, the scents of spring following refreshing rain, a haze of heat or autumn's golden glow.

Winter's Carpet, Posbury
Pastel, 250x325mm

The paintings illustrated here tell a compelling tale and express an essential truth in subject. Faithfully recording the fields and lanes of well-loved and well-tended landscape, the paintings will endure for generations as a remarkable testament to an artist who can not only truthfully transcribe but also express an empathy with the Devon landscape. There is romance here as well as observation, and an under-standing which passes beyond representation. Craftsmanship is also here abundantly, for these paintings are complex constructions and the observation hard won. For many years now Lionel has travelled across Europe and drawn inspiration from the hills, valleys and towns of France, Italy and Spain. The paintings here must also tell of a home-coming and an eye sharpened by the light beyond the Alps. Like many of his forebears in the great tradition of English landscape painting he seems to find constant renewal in the inspiration of his home county.

Many accolades have fallen on Lionel's shoulders from exhibiting with the Royal West of England Academy, the Pastel Society, the Royal Institute of Painters in Watercolour and the South West Academy. We are honoured that Lionel has chosen to exhibit the works illustrated in this book at our Devon gallery in Honiton.

So it is with great joy that I commend this book and all the paintings illustrated within to you, the viewer. This is an exceptional collection of work creating heirlooms for future generations; its inspiration drawn from city, town and field – a true expression of place.

Lionel Aggett is blessed with the eye and hand of a painter in harmony with his surroundings. This book is about the very heart of Devon and comprises memories and journeys that will touch the hearts of all those that love the West Country.

David Walker
Walker Galleries Ltd

INTRODUCTION

I consider myself fortunate to be earning my living solely through painting, working from my studio here in beautiful unspoiled Mid Devon: a wonderful man-crafted landscape between two widely different coasts and bordered by three counties each with their own distinctive character. It is here that Anne and I, married for thirty-seven years, have been happily settled for twenty-three years, since moving from nearby Exeter (Clyst St Mary). We are blessed with three grandchildren: our son Russell and his wife Lynn have Lucy; Kate our daughter, and her husband Trevor, have Lily and George. Anne also paints, specialising in cat paintings (past Chairman and President, now an honorary Life Member of the Society of Feline Artists.) Her studio is in the roof; mine is at the bottom of the garden.

This land of plenty, situated just off the north-eastern edge of Dartmoor where I was born, is the inspirational force which drives me to portray my local heritage, and the spark which kindles the desire to travel well beyond the county to experience and record the vastly different qualities of light and landscape to be found abroad. These journeys are always made with the knowledge that the sublime patchwork spread over nature's folds all around the studio like a vast textile tapestry, awaits my return.

I had always wanted to paint full time, but it was some while before my ambition was realised. This was however a period during which many experiences, including the creative, disciplined and professional practice of architecture under the watchful eye of the Royal Institute of British Architects, helped to forge an understanding of the methodology required in order to facilitate a successful application of the arts. Just as importantly, one was exposed to the harsh rigours of the professional business world, and the realities facing life in general, at a far earlier stage than had I attended art school. There is no substitute for living life at the sharp end!

Mid Devon Landscape (Nr Cadeleigh)
Pastel, 325x500mm

THE FORMATIVE YEARS

A Devonshire lad and proud of it, I was born in an old cob-and-thatched farmhouse at Whiddon Down beneath the backcloth of the rounded Cosdon Hill on Dartmoor, and with distant views of the western commons on Exmoor to the northeast. What a privileged start to enter the world in clear intoxicating country air; no wonder I have a penchant for wide dramatic vistas!

My father George ran his own garage and charabanc business. He built the garage himself and the covered forecourt to the petrol pumps still stands at the top of the hill. His pride and joy was a bull-nosed Morris vehicle, which ran down to Fingle Bridge and the gorge. My mother Marjorie opened up the farmhouse (now demolished) for bed and

Spinsters' Rock, Drewsteignton
Pencil, 210x297mm

Whiddon Down
Pastel, 250x325mm

breakfast and offered hot home-cooked meals to passing motorists on this the main route into Cornwall. She had her first customer within an hour of putting up the sign and business was then so brisk she sold both hers and my father's portions too! Although motoring was extremely popular, the pony and trap was often used for the trip to Exeter.

Dad's home was in Drewsteignton (the name Aggett is prevalent on this edge of the moor), in the beautiful old thatched house still known as 'Netherton', on the left as you climb the hill towards the sublime square with fine granite church, lychgate, thatched cottages and renowned Drewe Arms. He boarded at Queen Elizabeth School, Crediton, where Russell and Kate too received their education.

My mother, a Langman, was of Devonshire and Cornish stock from above the banks of the Tamar at Bere Alston, and a wonderful family of ten, so my brother Reg and I have many cousins! Sadly, we do not all keep in touch as well as we might, but the years of growing up together were magical and we were very close, more like brothers and sisters than cousins. My maternal grandmother, came from St Dominick on the Cornish side of the river, and the region was known for its fruit and flowers, particularly daffodils, and still is. Uncle Harry Langman was the last of the family to actively grow this beautiful flower for a living as part of his nursery business, on the steep slopes of the valley; truly backbreaking work. My grandparents lived with their large family in the terraced cottage below the old baker's where Sunday roasts were communally and sensibly cooked for the villagers. I can still recall the taste of the potatoes even now, a treat when we visited.

Apparently, my brother Reginald, who was seven when I came into this world, remarked that I behaved as a lion cub, always trying to escape from the depths of my cot. So I was christened Lionel in the

'Netherton', Drewsteignton
Watercolour, 230x310mm

Tamar Daffodils, Bere Alston
Pastel, 250x325mm

Church of St Mary the Virgin, Throwleigh
Pencil, 254x356mm

granite church of St Mary the Virgin, at Throwleigh, nestling beneath Shilstone Tor, Common and Hut Circle. The stones have always drawn me to their presence, which, whether hand-crafted or naturally formed through erosion, provide the backbone and structure of the timeless Dartmoor landscape.

Landscape is the function of structure, process and time

William Davies

The Second World War intervened and my parents sold the business and moved to Heavitree, Exeter in 1940. Dad was away most of the time, helping with the war effort as a Spitfire mechanic, although we saw more of him when he was stationed with the Spitfire Squadron at RAF Exeter.

The early formative years at Second Avenue were eventful and some-times exciting, to say the least. I suppose I can credit myself with a fair degree of imagination which, even though I had only three years' life experience, fully served to heighten the sense of impending danger and possible extinction. The sounds, and visual effects caused by the 19 air raids on the city between August 1940 and May 1942 are firmly etched in my memory. The eerie ascending and descending wail of the siren warning of the imminent night-time raids, awakened me in my cot, along with the sound of my mother's footsteps racing up the stairs to transport me down to the shelter in the dining room. This was a steel structure which doubled as a table with crossbars to

Bere Alston
Watercolour, 254x355mm

Dining Room, 7 Second Avenue
Pencil/watercolour, 210x297mm

the sides, through which my brother and I were confronted by the backs of women's legs, some with lines drawn by markers to depict American nylons (those without them), whilst they drank tea. We seemed to attract neighbours, both for shelter and comfort;

Mr Tucker's Garage Door
Watercolour, 355x254mm

my mother was renowned for that. One night we lost five houses immediately above us; the whistles of the bombs shrilled loud and clear above the throbbing of the Junkers 88 bombers. They say if you can hear the whistle, then it is not for you, and so it proved that night! There were times when we slept in the shelter, and I remember one Christmas, the sound of baubles crashing onto the steel sheet top from our Christmas tree as we arose, cracking our heads on the underside!

One Monday morning Reg and I were playing in the garden whilst Mum was hanging out the washing, the same exercise being repeated down through the other gardens. The rear gardens of Second and Wyndham Avenues are separated by a concrete surfaced alley, which served as our 'football and general sports' area. Mr Tucker's garage door at the top and outside our back gate formed the goal, much to his annoyance whenever a shot was skied into his orchard. His house loomed tall and ghostly behind.

All bedlam suddenly broke loose, the high whine of aircraft approaching at speed, and looking up we could see the cannons spitting death from the wings of all five Focke Wolfe 190s as they came in low from the direction of Woodbury sandpits, down over Heavitree and straight for us! We were bundled indoors and underneath the stairs by mum in almost one movement as cannon shells exploded and ricocheted off roofs and garden walls. Miraculously, no one was injured in our street, for when we eventually re-emerged, the washing all the way down through was in shreds. An unexploded shell was found in our garden afterwards, where Dad's neat rows of vegetables were decimated. A helmeted warden took the shell away in a bucket of sand. Trophies from similar and heavier raids such as shrapnel and shell cases were much prized by my elder brother and his gang!

I was sent to convent school, at the tender age of three and a half, for I had begun to develop the desire for exploration and travel. I had driven my poor mother to distraction, the final straw being my escape from the garden with my mate Michael Yandel, who lived at the corner shop in Ladysmith Road, both sharing a pedal car. We were missing for a whole day, with a police search team looking for us, as were

Air Raid by Five Focke Wolfe 190s
Watercolour, 305x406mm

'The Devastation' (High Street)
Pencil, 210x297mm

friends of both parents! We explored the outer regions of Heavitree Park, Hamlin and Sweetbriar Lanes, and were eventually discovered in Honiton Road by my Aunt Edith (Dad's sister) who at the time lived in St Loyes Road.

The Palace Gate Convent was bombed and so we were moved to Heavitree Convent. I can't say I enjoyed it all that much for I was always getting into trouble, sometimes deservedly (for cutting off the curls of the girl who sat in front of me during handicraft lessons for instance); at others not, when I nevertheless seemed to get the blame, due to my reputation no doubt! I can remember complaining to my mother that 'Surely if the nuns were allowed to play with their beads during prayers, then why couldn't I too misbehave just a little?'

I have a firm visual recollection of the vast emptiness of the city centre, viewed from the comfort of my pushchair, the mountains of bricks flanking paths and roads, their ordered layout seemingly pointless and without reason amongst the desolation where there were no buildings between. Where half-destroyed structures remained their window fenestration was replaced by fireplace openings staring out from exposed chimney-breasts. I remember the heat and swirling brick dust clouds of summer; a wonderful model aircraft flying (control line) display on the huge bomb-site of the Lower Market; the Black Watch band performing at the tented trade fair on the Sidwell Street bomb-site (most on offer seemed to be bottles of remarkable cleaning, decorating, staining and dying agents). I had all their autographs, later swapped for Dinky toys, later exchanged for other desirables, and so on. Then there was the lingering smell of old plaster, mortar dust and burnt timber, perfumed with rampant buddleia and convolvulous attracting colourful butterflies everywhere.

VE Day eventually came, followed by VJ Day. We collected our commemorative mugs during the community celebrations held at Ladysmith School hall and playground. I eagerly said yes with gusto when offered mustard with my American-style Hot Dog; a traumatic initiation to other new culinary experiences which lay just around the corner … dried eggs, bananas, barley sugar, sherbet and ice-cream.

The '99 Steps'
Pencil, 210x297mm

Orcombe Rocks, Exmouth
Watercolour, 254x355mm

Dad was back home more often and the wheels were put back on the Austin, jacked up 'in mothballs' inside our garage for the duration of the conflict. We were able to venture out using our rationed petrol to visit relatives and old friends at Drewsteignton, Whiddon Down, and Mill Farm where one of 14 cats used to lift the latch of the pantry door from the adjoining window-sill, whilst the remainder pushed it open, the clotted cream inside, their target! Uncle Ernest, ex-RAF, and Aunt Edith moved from St Loyes to Duryard where they started a market garden. There was no electricity and I can still smell the paraffin lamps across the supper table. Plenty of walks too, up the 99 steps to Hill Barton and the open countryside, and also the train to Exmouth from Polsloe Bridge Halt. The family at Bere Alston were visited, and the holidays at Looe where we stayed with Uncle Harold Stevens, a true

Cornishman, and mum's sister Ena were a joy. They lived in a cottage high on chapel steps in East Looe. I can still smell the particularly heavy seaweed aroma of Hannafore beach as we slowly combed the shingle for cowrie shells with my cousin Gillian, who deputised as the sister I didn't have. Anne and I enjoyed the same exercise with our children as they now do with theirs.

It was Uncle Harold who, when they were holidaying with us, and Dad was away, took me to Bristol to see the Busby Babes play the Rovers in the FA Cup. Although Manchester United lost 4–0, Bristol throwing away the script, I have 'supported' the Reds ever since. Likewise Exeter City of course, now sadly relegated to the Conference, where I was taken by my father who had a season ticket, before making my own way to St James's Park with friends all round with rattles and cowbells!

I had by now passed the entrance exam to Exeter School Preparatory Department, and through the hard endeavours, wishes and ambition of our parents, followed my brother through grammar school education. He started at Hele's and went on to Allhallows, Rousdon as a boarder.

Fingle Bridge by George Aggett (1903–78)
Oil, 360x410mm

Netherton House by L.C. Devenish), was always an inspiration to me as I discovered an early longing and wholesome desire to paint. The view has changed, and where once stood the old green tea shack on the other side of the bridge, now stands the Fingle Bridge Inn, formerly owned and developed by Harry Price and family, and known as the Angler's Rest. A great country-sporting venue, Fingle Gorge is renowned for its walks, trout and salmon fishing, and perhaps more in the past, game shooting. Mr Price senior, the local angler and artist who painted with my father, knew the river like the back of his hand, and also shot with my uncle, Percy Stanbury, who was Clay Pigeon World Champion.

I enjoyed my school years, especially those in the Preparatory Department, where imaginative expressionism was encouraged, notably demonstrated when I presented our nature mistress with grass snakes and slow-worms from my coat pockets and a cardboard box, all without prior notice. The sight of her fearful attempts to reprimand me from the top of her desk will remain with me for ever!

Always my idol he excelled at sport, and gained distinction in Art, only, alas, to never pick up a brush again after he left school. He chose a career in the Devon and Cornwall Constabulary, as did others on the Langman side of the family. Uncle Harry was Chief Detective Superintendent, cousin Tom in the CID whilst Reg was Traffic Sergeant in the Traffic Division. He is now retired and an excellent picture framer.

We both drew our artistic leanings from our parents, with Mum both musically and through drama. Many concerts were attended, and the house was regularly the venue for choir practice. Dad painted during his years at Drewsteignton, eventually abandoning the brush to become a perfectionist at engineering. His oil of Fingle Bridge, hanging in the dining room (together with a pen-and-ink study of

Netherton by L.C. Devenish
Pen and ink, 125x175mm

It was at this time at the age of ten that I took along my first, and as I thought, saleable painting of merit to Worth's Gallery in the Cathedral Yard (Mol's Coffee House). I was very politely and kindly told to keep at it, but to wait and then try again in a few years time.

The main school was of course more structured, although lacking in the fine art curriculum compared with the encouragement and facilities available today, which are magnificent. I was 'B streamed' all the way through, not helped by contracting scarlet fever during the summer term in the third form. The whole school was placed in quarantine and I missed practically the whole term. I stayed down another year and everything was too easy at first. I fooled around and consequently lost my sense of direction. One plus point at this time, was the completion of my first *plein air* painting, a watercolour, having cycled out to Bickleigh Bridge with fellow 3B classmate Anthony Wheaton, an excellent budding artist. The view of the Fisherman's Cot from the opposite bank of the Exe is now much changed, with a flat-roofed extension all round.

Many of the buildings within my territory in Heavitree survived the war and the 'village' is still fairly intact. The Regency and Victorian red-brick and rendered terraces afford superb renovated accommodation, although the lack of garaging causes an acute on-street parking problem. The terraces behind South Lawn Terrace are quite bijoux now. My school pal Geoff Bird used to live here when his parents ran a corner store – providing an endless supply of cream biscuits! Monte-le-Grande, where we used to play football behind the privet hedge (now gone), with its mix of Exeter brick Edwardian and Victorian terraces, and elegant Regency-style town houses is very popular, as is Regent's Park where our son Russell and his family now live.

St Michael All Angels, Heavitree
Pencil, 210x297mm

Greenhay, 13 Exe Vale Road, Countess Wear
Pencil, 210x297mm

This lofty and airy position provides open views across the city, with church towers, notably those of the cathedral, and steeples breaking the skyline. I won't dwell on those '60s intrusions and the rather unimaginative budget-conscious postwar build. Out of view and to the southeast stands the fine tower of Heavitree church, the scene of one of my youthful escapades. The school model club permitted flying in the playing fields, adjacent to Barrack Road, provided there was some form of control, ie. limited flight duration. My pal John Rowland (later to join the RAF and become a Hercules flying instructor), and I, both sporting Pirates Free Flight 1.0cc model aircraft decided to 'chance our arms' and see how far they would go. Mine went up and up, almost out of sight, and then descended to the northeast as the slight wind temporarily abated, narrowly missing the church tower and eventually crashing into the churchyard trees. John's won hands down, managing to catch the wind, requiring some frantic tracking up Manston Terrace and down Magdalene Street where it made a dodgy three-point landing – well almost! There was little traffic in those days! 'Free Flight' was curtailed from that day on. We then mounted our engines onto specially designed propeller-driven model racing cars, which, untethered tended to run out of control. Perhaps an even greater danger to the public were attempts with Michael Vincent to collect hydrogen in our garage. (At that time you were able to purchase equipment over the counter from the chemist.) We twice created an explosion before we remembered a 'quiet blue flame' had to be achieved before collection. Our chemistry master, who knew nothing of our experiments, was horrified when we approached him with our problem!

My parents bought a larger house in Exe Vale Road, Countess Wear in 1952, a move which opened up a whole new chapter in my life. Hornet's Hockey Club, which I joined in their first year, on leaving school, had their pitch just over the hedge, and their HQ in the Tally-Ho. There was a host of new friends, skiffle (our Exe Valley Skiffle Group was a great success, performing regular gigs, including a BBC radio debut), cycle trips galore, fishing on the canal and river trips in Roger's 10ft dinghy powered by my 4hp twin Britannia outboard, renovated by my father. We used to set out from Countess Wear village by the mill leat at high tide, once reaching the open sea off Budleigh Salterton. For the most part, however, we enjoyed the beauty of the Exe Estuary, before calling in at the Turf Hotel, followed later by a fight back against the tidal race and moored boats at Topsham to Countess Wear, returning under darkness – and we used to worry about our children!

Approaching Storm, Turf, the River Exe
Watercolour, 204x255mm

Under the expert guidance of my art master Sidney Hazard, I became keenly interested in architecture and the history of architecture, in addition to fine art. Although desperately keen to paint, it seemed that my creative instincts were being naturally channelled towards architecture, a decent and responsible profession. I can understand the unease my parents felt regarding the uncertainty of the former, given the sacrifice they had made. I just managed to scrape together sufficient subjects (maths was not my strong point) to become a probationer of the Royal Institute of British Architects, and entered articles with J. Francis Smith & Partners, a firm of architects and surveyors with offices in Exeter and London Wall. The Exeter office was a delight, situated on the first floor of No. 5 Cathedral Close, a fine Georgian-Regency building – absolutely sublime.

It was at this time in the late fifties and early sixties that the yearning to travel with a paintbrush began. A hiking trip in 1958 to Norway with old school pal Graham Hill, and a study tour in 1959 (again hiking), train fare paid by my tutor employer J. Francis Smith, with fellow employee, student and friend David Rhys to Umbria and Tuscany. These were followed by RIBA design travelling scholarship awards to Venice in 1960, (again accompanied by David, this time riding pillion on my 1956 150cc Lambretta), and then to the Rome School over Easter in 1962. There were painting and sketching trips with Lambretta and tent to Cornwall too, notably St Ives and the West Penwith where I was soon captivated by the light and atmosphere, visiting studios and galleries. I still have the sketchbooks, and diary reports from these early 'foreign' trips, the forerunners of the working diaries I produce today.

I was elected a Member of the Royal Institute of British Architects in 1967, the culmination of the long, hard pressurised stint of study and practical drawing, especially from Intermediate to Final, in the London office. I had to do five nights a week at Kingston School of Art and Architecture, plus drawing up through half the night and at weekends, plus Friday day release. The Royal Institute's course, combined with that of the College, provided a thorough grounding in the History of Art and Architecture, Fine Art, drawing, sciagraphy, perspective, design and all the associated practical and necessary technical subjects. But it was a truly memorable experience, relieved by Saturday-afternoon hockey, and evening highjinks at Merton Hockey club.

No. 5 Cathedral Close
Watercolour, 355x254mm

Stave Church, Near Norheimsund, Norway
Charcoal, 356x254mm (1958)

Doge's Palace, Venice
Ink, 254x356mm (1960)

Hilger & Watts Factory, Margate. Mural   Oil 1964 2100x5100mm

EXAMPLES OF STUDENT WORK

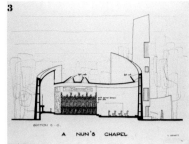

Left: *Kingston SAA Covent Garden 'Redevelopment'* Balsa model 1963

Right: *St Luke's Church, Countess Wear, Exeter* Oil 1959 1200x1800mm

School   Pencil 1955

Kingston SAA Design Study. Nuns' Chapel 1962

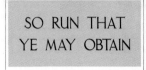

SO RUN THAT YE MAY OBTAIN

RIBA Intermediate Testimony of Study Lettering 1958

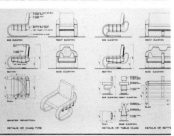
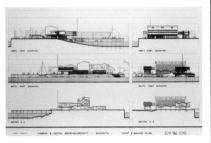
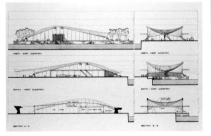

Right: *RIBA Intermediate Testimony of Study 1958. History sheet no. 3 – Medieval*

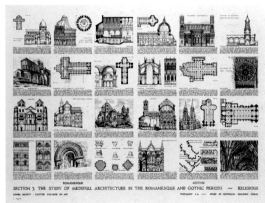

Top: *RIBA Final Thesis Design. Redevelopment of Exmouth Dock* Balsa model 1964

Above: *Dock Area. Furniture for Yacht and Sailing Club*

Top: *Dock Area elevations. Yacht and Sailing club*

Above: *Dock Area elevations. Sales and Service Building*

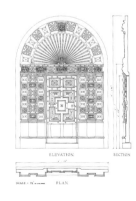

Left: *RIBA Intermediate Testimony of Study. Door to Bishop's House, Cathedral Close, Exeter* Measured drawing 1959

MARRIAGE, ARCHITECTURE AND ART

I met Anne in 1964 just after I returned from London to the Exeter office to complete my thesis, on the redevelopment of Exmouth Docks. It was love at first sight at our (Roger, David and me) joint birthday party in the hops bar at the renowned Bridge Inn, Topsham; at least, it was for me. I think Anne was eyeing up someone else! She was working in the City Library, and for several weeks thereafter the books on architecture and fine art were constantly being issued by this lovely girl. She said 'Yes' at the Ness, Teignmouth, by moonlight after a meal at the Passage House Inn, and then from one romantic location to another where one-and-a-half years later we were married in the cliff-top church at Lynton on the north coast. Anne moved there with her parents from Walton-on-Thames in 1963; she was born at Cheltenham on the edge of the Cotswolds, an area now much frequented by us both.

The Ness, Teignmouth
Watercolour, 178x254mm

The Bridge Inn, Topsham
Watercolour, 305x406mm

I had by now graduated from the Lambretta to a 1937 two-seater Morris Eight Tourer with canvas hood, and drop-down windscreen. Father renovated the engine, and I helped with the restoration and did the paint-work – five coats 'wet and dry', the colour flame red! Lulu was a peach.

We lived for a year in the Warberries, Torquay, whilst I worked for Edward Narracot & Partners, following a spell with Marshman & Warren in Looe Street, Plymouth, and having left J. Francis Smith to gain wider experience. I have much to thank J.F.S. for. He taught me discipline, the need for a professional approach to whatever you are doing, and also gave me his encouragement to pursue my painting in tandem with architecture. The last project I completed before leaving his office in order to broaden my experience was a 2.1 x 5.4m (7 x 18ft) mural in oils, for the then Hilger & Watts Instrument Manufacturers, whose factory we designed at Margate. Sir Edward Heath (then Minister of Trade) cut the tape.

The Church of St Mary the Virgin, Lynton, from the Foreshore, Lynmouth
Watercolour, 254x355mm

Cleeve Hill, the Cotswolds
Pastel, 250x325mm

Then followed five years in Truro, Cornwall, with the County Council, where I was able to produce both architecture and paintings including mural work, before taking up a post as Architect Planner with Exeter City Council, before going into private practice as equal partner (Radford Cruse Aggett Partnership). More interesting work, paintings and murals included, for the six years I was partner. Then came ten years with Exeter City Council as a Senior Architect, a period encompassing several schemes in which I involved the Art College where sculptures were installed by students and head of sculpture Roger Dean in specifically designed situations. My excursions to Italy many years earlier had impressed upon me the importance of bringing architecture, painting, notably murals, and sculpture together as one, in design, and not applied afterwards as an embellishment, or afterthought. Until recently we have not seen enough of this consideration which at most requires an extra one per cent on the budget.

We moved firstly to Clyst St Mary village when we left Cornwall, before the M5 and electricity pylons changed the local character somewhat. The motorway working provided many dramatic studies for paintings and I produced several works along the River Clyst looking across the meadows to the tranquil setting that was!

Dovers Hill, the Cotswolds
Pastel, 335x435mm

EXAMPLES OF ARCHITECTURAL WORK

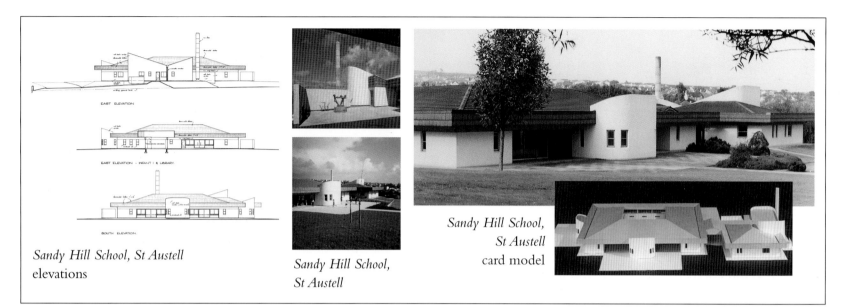

Sandy Hill School, St Austell
elevations

*Sandy Hill School,
St Austell*

*Sandy Hill School,
St Austell*
card model

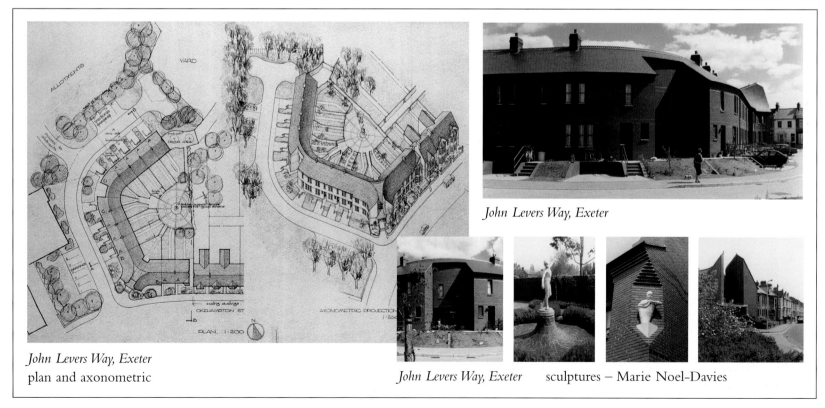

John Levers Way, Exeter
plan and axonometric

John Levers Way, Exeter

John Levers Way, Exeter   sculptures – Marie Noel-Davies

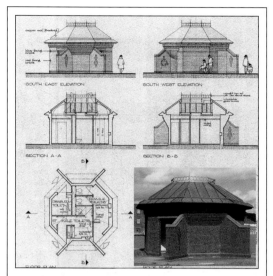

Exwick Public Toilets plans, elevations, sections

Wonford Housing, Exeter
sculptures by Roger Dean

Wonford District Centre
sculptures by Roger Dean

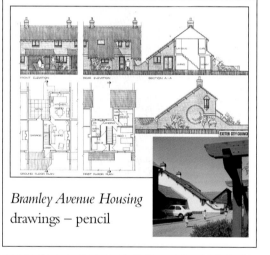

Bramley Avenue Housing
drawings – pencil

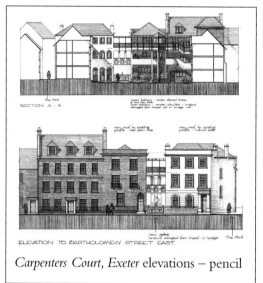

Carpenters Court, Exeter elevations – pencil

Exeter Quayside
Cannons and paving outside Custom House

*Building Society
Offices, Penzance*
mural & sculptures

Above left: *The Cheffers House, Topsham,* axonometric projection Design
development stage   Above right: elevations

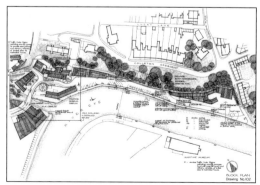

Exeter Quayside
plan, conservation study

THE REALISATION

So to Crediton in January 1980, so cold the removal van would not start, and our current location at the top of George Hill, with views to the east, south and west, the hills of Whitestone, Posbury and Dartmoor spectacularly lit at sunrise and sunset. The first ten years here turned out to be the last period for me as a 'practising' architect, for in 1990 my goal of painting for a living was finally realised. For a year I worked part-time to 'test the water', and then jumped ship altogether at the end of March 1991 to become a full-time professional artist.

Let me clarify, lest aspiring artists be seductively led to believe that it just simply happened like that – drop the 'T' square one day, and pick up a brush the next. I had been seriously drawing the two strings of my bow for some twenty-three years prior to this move, my first one-person show being held at Truro Galleries in 1968. It was a sell-out, and I remember not being able to sleep a wink that night following our celebratory drink with the gallery owner following the private view. I really thought, 'this is it'. Reality dawned during the course of the next few days. Discussions with my architect colleagues (we were working on some very interesting design solutions at the time), and repeated calculations on how one could survive and support a young family (Russell and Kate were born in Truro), dictated that I remained for the time being a working architect …

Moving to Cornwall, however, with my loving wife Anne who supported my painting, proved to be an inspirational decision, for I painted and painted at every opportunity. I am also indebted to Alan Groves, County Architect at that time, for the encouragement he gave me, to use my artistic talents in conjunction with architectural work where murals and sculptures (by Ron Wood of Mount Hawke, St Agnes) took their rightful place as an intrinsic part of architecture. To top this, project architects had to 'sign' their buildings in the form of a commemorative tablet, as an artist would a painting, leaving no doubt as to who was responsible for their creation!

Mid Devon Sunset, from Studio
Pastel, 325x250mm

Several one-person shows followed my early success at Truro Galleries, and this development continued when we moved to Exeter. I submitted work to open exhibitions organised by South West Arts, Civic Societies, Councils, Westward Television and companies such as English China Clays, and managed to win some awards. Showing at the Royal West of England Academy and Royal Institute of Painters in Watercolours helped, and I have exhibited with the Pastel Society since 1982, with over 40 works shown, entailing much graft to submit a full complement of paintings (six), transporting them to London, in the early days by public transport. My real break came when I sold well at their exhibition in 1990, including work to Manya Igel, the London dealer who continues to purchase paintings for her collection. As a result of this success I was approached following the exhibition by three London galleries who wished to present my work. This happily

Studio/Gallery

coincided with my decision to work part-time for a year. The Llewellyn Alexander Gallery, opposite the Old Vic Theatre, is where I decided to place my work, and I have shown there permanently ever since, having one-person exhibitions in November every other year. The gallery is small, huge in stature, very friendly, highly organised and, importantly, very successful, with a good clientele. Jillian Llewellyn-Lloyd (Managing Director), Ernest Chew (Chairman), and their team gave me immense encouragement from the very start.

The submission of work to art societies requires a certain approach. You have to accept that it is after all a lottery, for all the paintings could be at the same high standard, whereas only 300 or so can be accepted and hung, including all those presented by full members. There is heartache and jubilation, and participants have to accept the outcome and, if disappointed, just grin and bear it, then try again. The Federation of British Artists and the Pastel Society both set me firmly on my feet!

I am, happily, a 'free spirit' working with eminent galleries in London and the Provinces who regularly hold one-person and shared exhibitions of my paintings. In addition to Llewellyn Alexander I exhibit at the West End Gallery, W.H. Patterson, The John Davies

Clyst St Mary   Exhibited Pastel Society, 1982
Pastel, 150x150mm

The handwritten diary text in the sketch reads:

Thursday 27th July.

One hour in the studio and then meeting with the contractor to discuss progress & revised completion date - 18th August!! Then meeting with Appeal Blinds rep - natural wood slats - may be too heavy for perfect combination - investigate alternatives!

On with the painting of Florence - good session until 6pm - then evening meal whilst Kate & Trevor off to Russell & Lynnes - dinner with Richard and Annie Mdd.

This sketch from the new balcony above conservatory and overlooking garden and studio towards Q.E.S. lower school and Whitestone hills. Sue and Steve Sims called. Good chat - then correspondence - & walk with Anne. full day!

Studio from Balcony. Diary, Thursday 27 July   Watercolour, 200x200mm x 2

Gallery, Stow-on-the-Wold, The Clifton Gallery, Bristol, Sarah Samuels, Chester, The Walker Galleries at Harrogate and Honiton and Cove's Quay Gallery, Salcombe, and as a member of ST.ISA at St Ives. We did in the 1990s organise our own exhibitions (four) in the Clarence Hotel, Exeter, where we 'converted' the Clarence Room into a gallery with professional shop-fitting stands designed and supplied by Geoff Fletcher (Crystal Designs), our friend in Crediton. We also show here at the Studio, where Phase Two of our alterations and extensions will hopefully be underway this year, providing more hanging space (I have finally managed to design something for ourselves). Organising publicity, invitations, private views and hanging paintings correctly, gives a good insight for artists, an indication as to what good galleries

do for you. All should try it, then there might be less of a tendency to gripe at the percentage take, which, granted, can be very high.

Moderate success can sometimes be achieved by walking the pavements, but most galleries have their own agenda and hit list. You may be lucky to meet the right dealer in the right place at the right time or, as I did, through the auspices of a Society. Whichever the method, a great deal of hard work is required. Paintings must be well framed and delivered to a high standard, maintaining a high level of consistency throughout. To achieve this on a regular basis you must possess the drive, discipline and the will. Painting for a living is hardly totally relaxing, so often the taunt, but enjoyable it certainly is, even

Wednesday 2nd August.
Full day in the studio - completed the "Arno, Florence" and started on the Restaurant I Minerva, Assisi - interesting composition looking through umbrellas with columns of temple forming contrasting vertical element accentuated by tower rising above horizontal table & chairs element. Poppies Newlyn, shown in this sketch of studio in progress. Prepared Living Room floor, ready for floor layers / sanders to morrow.

Studio!

Studio Interior. Diary, Wednesday 2 August
Watercolour, 200x200mm x 2

House/Studio Extension (Phase One) Sculpture,
'Cradle Song' by Witold Gracjan Kawalec.

when contracted to produce 60 works for a major show. There is never quite the same 'edge', however, as that experienced by an architect when taking on a very large commission for which he, as an insured professional, is fully responsible to his client, and where his property, along with those of his partners, is required as collateral. Not all architectural contracts run smoothly once the design work is completed, as the above observations imply, whereas the artist is indeed fortunate that the finished painting is uniquely his or hers alone.

Whilst this book is being produced, artists are increasingly using the web to sell direct. Sites that can provide cross-references with reputable galleries will provide potential clients with sound knowledge with regard to an artist's long-term status and consistency, particularly where artists and galleries work together.

HERITAGE

Making a living through expressing in two-dimensional form, the attributes of a heritage that many would give up everything to share, is indeed a rewarding existence. Several do head southwestwards of course, as portrayed in the BBC TV Series 'Down to Earth'. Whole lifestyles are changed to settle here, swapping the heavy concentrations of the greater metropolis for clean air breathed amidst glorious scenery. It is no accident of nature that rare mosses which only thrive in the purest atmospheres have re-established themselves on Dartmoor. It does not work for everyone, as many have found out, and the opportunities for finding work and the various physical problems to be encountered can be difficult, particularly if you intend to work from the land itself. You have to know and respect the countryside, and if you are new to all the vagaries of the different and changing moods, and the extreme conditions it can hurl at you, then in order to cope you have to learn and adapt. The mere donning of green wellington boots will not guarantee survival.

As an artist drawing inspiration from the results of man's endeavours to root out a living from the land, it assists the creative flow to have a knowledge of how we have tamed and shaped the landscape, as indeed a portrait painter needs to get inside his subject's head to produce a 'living work'. There is evidence everywhere of man's contribution to the forging of such beauty. Some areas are loosely garlanded with the term 'wilderness', but even here we have had a considerable bearing on the outcome. Take Dartmoor, for example, where man has recently orchestrated a change in appearances, not by hand, but through his management of animals and grazing. As a result, ferns are taking over vast areas. Habitats can be drastically altered through changes in land management and farming practices. Whereas Dartmoor was once a deciduous forest supporting deer, wolves, wild cats, and woodcock, it is now a changed but nevertheless still glorious landscape of high rugged tors capping great heaving swathes of heather, bracken, grasses and ferns, with deep contrasting clefts. Here, clear moorland streams race between moss-covered granite boulders, jumbled amidst remnants of the lichen-covered stunted oaks of the ancient forest. Intruding into this landscape is the myriad of patchwork fields so typical of Devon and Cornwall and, not so long ago, Brittany in France. Spreading out in all directions from the moor, the earth of these small enclosures changes from a peaty burnt umber, and northeastwards gradually to raw umber through to the Mid Devon red earths. These tracts of vibrant fiery soil surround Crediton, our house and studio, as we look south across to Whitestone, Posbury, and southwest to the moor. It is a glorious landscape for which we are all thankful, and proud to share as our heritage.

High Summer, Chapel Down (Redlands)
Pastel, 250x325mm

CREDITON

'If we ever decided to move to Crediton and the Mid Devon area this is precisely where I would like to be'…'Me too,' echoed Anne. So ran the conversation, or approximately so, back in 1966 as we leaned over the gate at the top of George Hill, having parked nearby, beside Upper Deck, a viewing platform from where you can see Dartmoor to the southwest, and way across Mid Devon towards Exmoor to the northeast. It is known, aptly, as Redlands for the soil is a fiery red, particularly when dry and reflecting the warm evening sunlight. Little did we know, that fourteen years later we would indeed move to Crediton, just below and yards from where we were standing. Our move in 1980 proved to be a pivotal point in our lives; a change of job and access to a very good school, Queen Elizabeth, Crediton, for Russell and Kate.

In truth, as an Exonian I had always considered Crediton, particularly when in private practice, as a place to drive through to and from

High Street, Crediton   Watercolour, 204x255mm

Farmers' Market. Diary, Saturday 4 March   Watercolour, 200x200mm x 2

projects in North Devon, either to meetings or on my way back to the office to sign post and always held up by traffic. Consequently, many an unsavoury word was uttered under my breath in Crediton High Street. It is also true that many cycling trips were enjoyed in my younger days, notably to play cricket at that perfect gem of a ground, Shobrooke. The Exe Valley was however a more popular cycle ride, probably because of the easier gradients, as was the natural gravitation to the sand and sea of the south coast, notably the 'Warren'.

The saying 'Crediton was a cathedral town when Exeter was a fuzzy down' is often repeated as a friendly riposte against the eventual and historical development of the latter compared to that of the Mid Devon market town.

Crediton has lost its street cattle market and wonderful market with bow-fronted units at the four corners. Two of these remain, the overall space currently half obliterated by the Fire Station which, together with our superb fire-fighters and resuscitation unit, is thankfully to be moved to another site, thus enabling the valiant efforts of Crediton's 'Square Action Group' to be realised. This is a focus for the town, a square where functions, events and extended markets can be held, and where townsfolk and country folk can pause awhile. 'Kirton' does, through the inherent geniality of its inhabitants, encourage both newcomers and locals alike to participate in informal encounters at every corner and along the length of High Street. Saturday morning shopping sessions are a particular joy for those not in a hurry, and if you can organise your routine so that you

The Green. Diary, Saturday 29 April

Watercolour, 200x200mm x 2

Cockles Rise. Diary, Saturday 24 June

Watercolour, 200x200mm x 2

are not short on time, then unwind whilst catching up on the news and procuring the weekend fare.

Although it cannot claim to be 'beautiful' it is, as one would expect of a thriving working community, collectively full of character, and possessing several delightful cameos. It is this slight edge and rounded rawness which time and again compels me to wander out with my sketchpad/diary to record the unsung delights of this friendliest of towns.

Nestling at the bottom of the very steep and long George Hill from our house and studio is the Green, a wonderful space where fairs used to be held. It is occupied by three magnificent trees, two horse chestnuts, one pink-flowered, one cream, and a copper beech amongst others, and flanked by cottages along Kiddicot, and my local, the Duke of York, and Bill and Di Fox's Restaurant, The Grapevine on the other side of the

road. Bill and Di do not advertise their bistro-style restaurant, they're that good, and enjoyable evenings with good food and ambience, their trademark, are conveniently followed by a steady and safe climb home!

Although Crediton is surrounded by beautiful and luxuriantly rich countryside with delightful footpaths, it does also boast two excellent green spaces, People's Park and Newcombes Meadow. Both offer exceptional vistas, the former down and across the town and from the other the fine church and surrounding hills.

Numerous courtyards and narrow streets leading off the main street (where the April Great Markets were held), afford an insight to the town's original character. North Street, Dean Street, and Cockles Rise are notable examples, and where I have set up my easel on many occasions.

MID DEVON

It was, therefore, undoubtedly the sheer natural beauty and unspoiled working nature of the landscape surrounding Crediton that turned our observation back in 1966 into reality. The whole of Devon is beautiful in its sheer diversity, and one could settle anywhere here and be content. Our decision was, however, absolutely the right one for us and the children. Their upbringing amongst their and our friends, all within walking distance of the school, maximised and provided for full participation in all things local. Add to this the unbelievable source

of inspiration to be gleaned from the complementary red and green landscape, and you have 'paradise'!

I have already referred to the excellent footpath system around Crediton, affording views across the town and out into the surrounding landscape, so where better to start than mention the newly formed pedestrian connection with Sandford, providing a safe link between the town and its attractive neighbouring village, to the northeast and vice-versa. The access is completely free of traffic apart from the crossover of the Barnstaple Cross lane behind us, and that by Creedy

Monday, 31st. August.
Worked on the "Arno From The Uffizi - shaping up well and Jillian will come down to select paintings for the off to Italy tomorrow for a tour of the opera in the drawers etc. - gradually getting things straight! This walk in the fields above us and a "playground" of imag ination and make-believe for Russell, Kate & their friends !! ..

loose treatment. Confirmed with Ernest by phone that he catalogue in early September. Glad I phoned - they are Marche below Venice. Anne sorted out a few more sketch, after supper, to the right of our favoured wood

Top Field. Diary, Monday 31 August   Watercolour, 200x200mm x 2

Landscape Between Crediton and Bickleigh Diary, Friday 5 May

Watercolour, 200x200mm x 2

Lodge. The prime motivation for the construction of this path came from the village, owing to the lack of a pavement on the increasingly busy road. The very fine result has also created an excellent amenity for the people of Crediton. A very pleasant walk takes you through woods flanking fields with views across typical Mid Devon country-side, aflame with rich red soil, past Frogmire and along the stream-fed meadow leading into Sandford. Here the choice of a drink in either first, the Rose and Crown, on the left, or the Lamb Inn in the square, awaits you before the return trip or continuation to West Sandford or Upton Hellions, making a circular walk.

My main source of inspiration comes from the amazing stretch of red-enriched landscape running roughly from Hittisleigh on the Two Moors Way to Bickleigh in the Exe Valley. High ridges along this stretch of countryside give wondrous views across a heaving patch-work of small fields, the colours of which change according to the farmer's yearly work programme and the seasons. Even the same season brings changes each year, with different crops being introduced and general rotation.

The most sensational effect of the complementary red and green comes during May, when the fresh, vibrant new growth of the grasses, cereals and foliage contrasts with the ploughed fields, some with bright-green new shoots appearing in neat rows to add scintillating

Mid Devon (from Windwhistle Corner)
Pastel, 175x175mm

painted the view several times, under different conditions during all four seasons, and it still draws me back time and again. I shall never tire of the sheer majesty and atmosphere of the place. There is gradual change too, with tree planting on the near hillsides. Subjects abound all along this stretch and my interpretations of them appear later in the book.

We have all been asked at some time or another, which is our favourite season? Certainly, with regard to painting they are all equal in my book. In their cycle the beauty and secrets of each is gradually revealed, and we are again treated to individually contrasting displays, perhaps temporarily forgotten during the enjoyment of the preceding months. When assessing their visual qualities, however, the splendour of the particular season under discussion can quickly promote it to number one, until the next, and so on.

Perhaps it is my general optimism that encourages me to welcome with open arms, the newness, freshness and promise that spring brings each year, the season that comes so early in this part of the country. One of the first signs, the snowdrop, provides some wonderful displays around us, followed by the daffodil and then the bluebell accompanied by a host of other wild flowers jostling to get in on the act. The grounds of the tiny, beautiful church of St Mary the Virgin, Stockleigh English, is awash with snowdrops in February, and as with all wild plants, some years are better than others. A fine lych-gate and the thatched Church Cottage provide a wonderful entrance to the small churchyard. In medieval times the pure white blooms of snowdrops were a symbol of Candlemas (2 February), the feast of purification of the Virgin Mary. My other favourite area for these 'snow piercers' (literal translation from their French name) are the woods flanking the Sandford walk, a huge cluster of especially strong larger specimens straddling the steep slope. Another and more famous location where I have painted snowdrops amidst a woodland setting is outside the county at Snowdrop Valley, below Wheddon Cross on Exmoor, sharing the spectacle with hundreds of other admirers!

perspective across their rolled and folded shapes. The sensation is further enriched under the warm evening sunshine, particularly after a dry spell.

This highly charged landscape spreads beyond this 'ridgeway' of course, extending southwest to Torbay and down through East Devon. It appears at its most magnificent perhaps at Windwhistle corner, west of Cadbury Castle. The view northwestwards from here over Cheriton Fitzpaine towards Stockleigh English and Woolfardisworthy is simply stunning. The multi-perspective of tiny fields spreads far out into Mid and North Devon. One feels Hartland Point is just over the furthest ridge, which on a clear day, with fine visibility, it certainly is. I have

At the end of this stretch of magnificent countryside at Bickleigh, lies another wonderful tract affording breathtaking views of the Exe Valley, through to Sidmouth Gap on the south coast. A narrow lane (part of the 'Exe Way') beyond Bickleigh Castle climbs steeply up to the ridge high above the west bank of the River Exe, before dropping down once more to river level at Thorverton. Pitt Farm nestling below, with the valley spreading out beyond has (and will continue to do so) been the subject of many paintings during all the seasons.

Posbury Clump, to the southwest of Crediton and seen from the studio, together with neighbouring Posbury Camp, is an area steeped in mystic and ancient history. The whole area exudes a special quality and atmosphere equalled by the natural beauty of the place. I have worked here often, more so in winter, resulting in several snow scenes. The ethereal nature is heightened by the quiet stillness that always accompanies a covering of snow, manifested at this location, by the nearby convent. This retreat from the hustle and bustle of modern day living embues a feeling of serenity and calm to all who climb the hill.

Posbury
Pastel, 175x225 mm

THE MOORS

I suppose it is more likely, taking into consideration my roots, and the proximity of our house and studios to Dartmoor, that we should gravitate to this huge pile of granite more often than the softer rounded Exmoor. In truth, I am very fond of both, but it is the 'land of my birth' that has so far attracted me the most, resulting in many paintings, some of which are reproduced here.

The two moors are quite different, but equally beautiful in their own way. Dartmoor is the more rugged, with hard 'sculptured' granite outcrops (Tors) rising high above the bracken, heather and grasses. Deep clefts support the remains of the ancient oak forest, rising through moss-covered granite boulders, similar to that found in Wistman's Wood. The harshness of winter accentuates and produces a 'sharp edge' to the tough granite formations, and against snow or frost the quartz takes on the mantle of cold steel. The encroachment of farming enclosures/fields has softened the moor at its outer edges, and penetrating through to areas such as Hexworthy, Widecombe, Babeny and Holne. I particularly like the contrast between the rough moorland and patchwork fields when viewed across the flanks of the moor and looking outwards.

The nearest part of the moor to the studio is the Steps Bridge access on the B3212, and so it is from Exeter. This area, running into the moor through Moretonhampstead, is the tract that, since a youngster, I have visited the most. The walk, from Steps Bridge along the Teign at the base of Dunsford wood to Clifford Bridge through glades of daffodils, is truly memorable. Walk further it you wish, to Fingle Bridge, for the Teign Valley Gorge is extremely beautiful; I am perhaps biased for my sentiments are firmly rooted there.

Moretonhampstead, although well within the National Park boundary, is still some distance from the unfenced moorland. It stands proud, the parish church aloft from the houses tumbling down the hill, a welcoming gateway to the 'wilderness' beyond. We enter this area at Leapra Cross and Moor Gate, climbing up to Shapley Common, where can be experienced the contrast between high moorland and the patterned farmland stretching away from the north west to the southeast. Hut circles beneath Shapley Tor make wonderful studies with the vast landscape spreading beyond. It is on these higher points of the moor, amongst the stones and near isolation, (more so further in), that one feels a presence. Whatever the mood surrounding them, and whether shaped, moved and re-erected by man, or simply sculpted over time by nature, the stones have an aura about them, an ability somehow to communicate with the past as well as – and importantly – look forward.

To the south, Hookney and Hameldown Tors rise above spectacular Grimspound, where 24 hut circles lie within the massive granite-stoned walls. Late evening, when you are more likely to be on your own, is when best to experience the 'vibes'. The views from this area, across Headland Warren towards the Warren House Inn, are breathtaking.

Continuing in a southerly direction the Bonehill area above Widecombe contains some majestic piles of granite, and particularly along the lane climbing from the village up to Bonehill there are some fine examples of granite dry walling, and wonderful boulders, some incorporated into the walls.

Honeybag, Chinkwell and Bell Tors all offer spectacular views. Bonehill Down overlooks Widecombe where dressed granite has so beautifully created the 'cathedral of the moor' church of St Pancras. A short distance away to the northeast, Hound Tor and surrounding hut circles plus the nearby characterful Bowerman's Nose on Hayne Down, have provided much source of inspiration. In contrast to these elevated places, Belstone Cleave and Skaigh Wood right on the most northern tip of the moor are steeped in mystery, where the River Taw tumbles out of the ground to embark on its journey to the north coast. Dark and green with mosses camouflaging the rounded boulders, the valley takes on a lighter air in the winter, the trees stripped bare at a time when you'd think they would need their 'clothing' the most, such is the depth of cold where the low sun departs early. All of the woods on the moor have their distinctive moods and character. Wistman's is more rugged, whereas Pencleave Wood above Okehampton caresses the small but striking castle rising high above the surrounding trees and West Okement River.

Little Mis Tor, Dartmoor
Pastel, 325x500 mm

Northeastwards from Wistman's Wood, and right in to the bare moor-land, stands the Beardown Man just west of Devil's Tor. To accompany this eerie menhir late in the day, is to experience the feeling of being somewhere near the edge! This perhaps has something to do with the proportions of the stone which vary in shape and stature depending from which side it is viewed.

To the west of Wistman's Wood and Beardown Tors rises the massive outcrop of Great Mis Tor, with Little Mis Tor below. This wonderful pile of granite, known as an avenue tor comprising several major blocks, on the western edge of the moor above Tavistock, is perhaps the most rugged and cathedral like, although I am not qualified to make such a judgement as I have yet to visit every tor! Our daughter Kate has climbed most, having trained for, and participated in, the excellent 'Ten Tors' youth challenge at all three levels.

It is the proliferation of huge weathered granite masses with horizontal and vertical fissures surrounded by clitter, the debris formed by frost action in the Ice Ages causing the solid core of the tor to disintegrate, that distinguishes this National Park from Exmoor, where the summits are gently rounded. Great Mis Tor with its extensive area of clitter, is

a superb example, and a compelling subject for me. The views out and down across Tavistock and well into Cornwall are stupendous.

Tucked beneath this western side of the moor below the A386 and north of Mary Tavy stands Wheal Betsy, proud testimony of the moor's mining industry.

Returning to the northeastern edge of the moor, the stone rows across Shovel Down have provided much material for me. Although they are located not very far into the moor, I was once during a February painting session surrounded by a thick, cold, swirling mist which descended over me and my easel frighteningly quickly. Wallabrook Bridge and Scorhill Circle are favourite subjects too, all painted under widely different conditions.

Exmoor will hopefully feature more in a future book. It is a quest of mine to paint along the course of the Exe from its source to the sea at Exmouth. The rounded hills of the moor, which pitch into the sea unlike those of landlocked Dartmoor, are illustrated by this view near the Somerset border.

Middle Hill, Exmoor
Pastel, 325x500 mm

EXETER AREA

Exeter will always be dear to me, not only as the place where I lived through my school days to adulthood, but where, as a happily married man with a wonderful wife and two great children, I was fortunate enough to be able to return and contribute in a modest way as an architect to the development of the city. To me Exeter is a red city, the natural red-clay brick and Heavitree stone relieved by the use of neutrals, ie. render and Beer-type stone here and there. It is a travesty that the ready availability of various coloured bricks and other materials, plus a lack of early stringent control, permitted a plethora of undesirable development in the late sixties and early seventies. The last twenty years has seen much-improved planning control, common sense and architectural good manners, regarding the correct choice of materials in respect of texture, colour and durability, resulting in a more indigenous but creative and forward-looking design.

Many of the paintings in this section have been produced over the last fifteen years with most of my recent activity, confined to Mid Devon, West Penwith and abroad.

The Canal Basin and Exe river-bank area of the city has recently undergone substantial changes, and there are many subjects to be found along the riverside park, immensely popular with locals for its recreational qualities, since coming to fruition. I am looking forward to producing more work along this stretch of the river as part of the Exe 'study' mentioned earlier. Meanwhile, the Exeter paintings in this book feature, in the main, the city centre, notably Southernhay and the Cathedral precincts, the 'Yard' and the 'Close'.

Southernhay has always attracted me, with its fine trees and simply but attractively laid-out gardens. A long rectangular space running north to south, flanked by red-brick Georgian houses (now offices) with fine delicate white-painted hardwood windows on both west and east sides, and elegant stuccoed Regency dwellings (also offices) in Southernhay East. The subtle effects produced by the play of light in Southernhay is attractive at all times of the day, during all four seasons: the midday winter sun shines low along the length of the 'Hay', just

Dix's Field
Pastel, 400x500mm

picking out the jambs and slim mullions of the windows, bright against the warm red of the brickwork, long shadows cast on the sometimes snow-covered grass; the sinewy long shadows of early spring, cast by trees shortly to don their summer clothes, encircled by crocus rings; summer itself, the now fully clad branches casting deep cooling shadows over office workers at their lunch boxes. So to autumn, and particularly the early morning sun, springing warm shafts of light across dew laden grass, sprinkled with golden leaves from the flame-coloured trees.

Our architects' practice was in Southernhay West, before we relocated to Cathedral Yard, just across from the Close where I began my architectural career. My memories of time spent in this lovely space are therefore manifold, through recovery from the blitz, the remembrance services attended with parents both inside and outside the magnificent cathedral, and school services. There is always something interesting happening; that is not to say my nose was always pressed to the office window during those articled student days, but watching some passers-by in their summer dresses was always a delight! There were comings and goings generated by the various services, commemorative events, concerts and all those things associated with the workings of a busy cathedral, the secular focus of the city and county. People have always naturally gravitated to the precinct, visiting players such as the Foots Barn Theatre performers, morris dancers, mothers with children taking five from shopping, lunch-breakers and, of course, holiday visitors. Most importantly, it was from the first-floor office window in the Close that I saw Anne standing on the Cathedral Lawn a few days after I first met her at the Bridge Inn, and proclaimed there and then that this was the girl I was going to marry. The building listed momentarily towards the cathedral as the entire staff moved to the window, eager to see who had moved this lad, who until that moment appeared to have only hockey and beer on his mind! All concurred on both points! Many paintings have evolved out of my love for this place, some rather architectural portrayals of the cathedral, the Yard and Close, others less so.

I have mentioned hockey and the way sport and outdoor activities generally have always helped to address the balance between work and

Cathedral of St Peter's in Exeter
Watercolour, 630x547mm

play. This has been important to me. Throughout all the studying and later application during the practice of architecture and now art, hockey particularly has been the safety-valve. My club, Hornets, amalgamated with Exeter and more latterly Culm Vale to become Exeter and Culm Vale Hornets (ECVH), with five men's and two women's teams of which I am proud to be President, and so the interest continues…

Competitive exercise is maintained in a modest way through golf which I have just taken up. A hockey painting is included, not of the club but of Exeter School v Blundell's School on the astro-pitch used by ECVH until recently, and one of the four paintings produced to assist the school's pitch fund organised by John Jago, Old Exonian and fellow Crossing House member. Further down Barrack Road is Wyvern Barracks, the home of the 43 (Wessex) Brigade, visited by the School Cadet Force for training and examination. I was reacquainted with the barrack square on Saturday 28 September 1991, when commissioned to paint the 'Presentation of New Colours to the 4th Battalion The Devonshire and Dorset Regiment (The 1st Rifle Volunteers) by the Colonel-in-Chief His Royal Highness The Duke of Kent KG, GCMG, GCVO, ADC'. The full-dress rehearsal for the event on the previous Thursday was performed under clear blue skies. Whilst choosing my position in the VIP stand from where I could best record the precise moment of the presentation, I remember one of my concerns was the vast area of parade ground which inevitably would be revealed through

Exeter from Telegraph Hill
Pastel, 500x650mm

painting the whole battalion as instructed. This particular problem was solved on the day when proceedings had already been delayed by heavy rain, whilst decisions were taken whether to wait for the forecast break, or to go ahead with back-up plans for a reduced ceremony under cover in the Drill Shed, and for which no painting would be commissioned. Just in time a parting through the cloud cover allowed the parade to get under way, only for the heavens to open once more, this time releasing torrential rain. The band wore capes, but the remainder of the contingent in their smart unprotected uniforms, including His Royal Highness, just soaked up the deluge! Yet everyone performed unflinchingly and impeccably. Meanwhile, the canvas roof of our VIP stand gathered water, until one bay at the rear split and soaked the guests below. Orderlies were quickly despatched with brooms to expertly ease the remaining ponding to the sides without further catastrophy. Throughout all this, a quiet genial and orderly humour was expressed. I have nothing but admiration for all concerned, and for the complete Britishness with which the whole situation was handled, both off and on the parade ground. The rain stopped for that 'precise moment', and my previous fears proved unfounded for the rain-soaked tarmac and puddles, produced broken reflections which added interest to an otherwise bland middle foreground. An artist's view surely, and at what cost?

Exeter is surrounded by red hills and generally these have been protected, providing glimpses of fields from the centre which is unique for a city of such size, giving credence to an observation made by some that visually it possesses the charm of a country town. Views from the surrounding countryside, too, show how comfortably Exeter nestles in the landscape. The most dramatic viewpoints are from the top of Haldon and Telegraph hills before the A38 (Plymouth) and A380 (Torbay) roads converge at the 'Woodlands' (now renamed Deer Park) base, once a country club frequented during my irresponsible youth. Beyond Peamore and closer to the city, one subject I have painted several times is the view of Knowle Hill, from the Waybrook on the Alphington Road. This very steep knoll featured 'prominently' at the start of our school cross-country runs. The gently sweeping curve of the small valley down past the hill, through to the Exe basin presents a strong almost 'abstract' composition, the components of which change markedly according to the season and crop planted.

Topsham has always featured in my life, from very early on when helping Uncle Ernest with his salmon net fishing by Newport House, which he did in conjunction with his market garden there, and later when painting the salmon fisherman at work mending their nets beneath the church wall. I love the contrast between the tight narrow alleys of the town, and the vast expanse to be enjoyed at its edge where the Exe widens out to become an estuary. Not far from here and on the River Clyst, which joins the Exe immediately below Topsham, Clyst St Mary provided much inspiration during the seventies. This is where we settled for seven years, making many friends, on our return from Cornwall before moving to Crediton. It is still an attractive village but many of my paintings were produced before the M5 and pylon-infested fields that came in the cause of progress. The new motorway, particularly, featured in my work at that time, the massive excavations and moving of enormous quantities of red earth by huge machines providing potent subject matter. The quieter and less dramatic corners also attracted my attention: the simple and often quite ordinary, at first glance, pastoral combination of field, river bank, mill, cottage and tree that inspired me to produce a whole series of small works, an approach to painting that I often apply today. There are things we see, or rather don't really see, and which are therefore taken for granted, but which offer extraordinary value to our well-being, when viewed and observed more closely, a thing we so naturally used to do as children.

Clyst St Mary
Conté, 211x254mm

BEYOND THE HEART

Broadly speaking, South Devon and the coast, particularly around the estuaries of the Teign and Exe, is softer and gentler than North Devon which is rugged, wilder and less developed, although the outcrops of Beer Head, Hope's Nose, Berry Head, and Bolt Head together with the most southerly Prawle Point, counter this generalisation. Here the South Hams has a distinctive character all of its own, and where Salcombe, the joy of my youth, and also the venue of family camping and boating holidays, provides a feast of subjects. Across to the eastern side of the county rise the Blackdown Hills, the site of three important airfields during the Second World War: RAF Culmhead (Church Stanton, where my father was based for a while) just over the border in Somerset, RAF Dunkeswell, and RAF Upottery (Smeatharpe). It was from the latter that the US 101st Airborne Division took off for the Cherbourg Peninsula on D-Day, on 6 June 1944. Perhaps the significance of that historic event has some special bearing on the incorporeal atmosphere, which clings in the air right across this 'plateau'. The landscape is also extremely beautiful, deep clefts diving steeply off the deciduously endowed summits, as can be seen from the A30 and A373 around Honiton. Here is a handsome town, benefiting from the bypass which affords easy access to a generous car park, with pedestrian access through a shopping precinct to the adjacent busy High Street and its street market held on Tuesdays and Saturdays. A striking parish church, good shops, pottery, lace, galleries and antiques provide subjects galore!

Broadhembury. Diary, 10 March

Watercolour, 200x200mm x 2

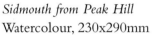

Sidmouth from Peak Hill
Watercolour, 230x290mm

North Devon Cliffs
Pastel, 175x225mm

Tarka Sheep, Taw Estuary
Pastel, 150x150mm

Broadhembury, midway between Honiton and Cullompton to the northwest and just off the A373 is perhaps the archetypal Devon village, a perfect assemblage of cob-and-thatched dwellings, with pub and church around the 'square'. In truth, there are happily many like this, but it is one of the finest examples that I have visited and painted. Sidmouth, due south on the coast, and right down to Paignton in Torbay, is where the red rolling hills meet the sea in strikingly red-sandstone cliffs which often stain the emerald sea a blood red, romantically expressing the injurious nature of constant erosion. At Sidmouth the 'Redwings' heighten the colourful spectacle, and I have made several studies of these boats, their sails echoed by the triangular cliffs running towards Beer Head. We regularly visit the Sidmouth Folk Fesitval where the brilliant formal events are almost equalled by the impromptu performances along the front and in the pubs.

There is a sharp contrast between these colourful soft crumbling shores of the south coast, and the treacherously and magnificently rugged west-facing coastline of North Devon around Hartland Quay and Hartland Point. These impressive cliffs, together with the Higher and Lower Sharpnose Points just over the border in Cornwall, are part of the same geological formation, which, through erosion has produced long parallel rows of jagged teeth stretching far out into the sea. On shore, the huge folded slabs rise and fall all along the coast like huge 'frozen' strata-borne waves, which is what they are. No one can fail to be impressed by the sheer power and strength of the uplift, which caused such a phenomenon. These great slabs present powerful and complex shapes, which through their majesty and the undoubted misery they have caused to shipping down the centuries, exude a feeling of awe, wonderment, and just a little *suave qui peut* to us mere mortals.

Eastwards beyond Hartland and Winbury Points, the cottages of Clovelly village tumble down steep, wooded cliffs to its quaint harbour, all well tucked into the lee, and away from the westerlies roaring in from the Atlantic. The views of the tranquil setting from high above along the Hobby Drive are especially romantic.

We often take our bikes to Barnstaple or Great Torrington to cycle the Tarka Trail, running along the route of the old railway line between the two towns. There are wonderful views across the estuary from Instow to Appledore, and the wide expanse of Saunton Burrows provides huge sky- and seascapes, in addition to being a favourite venue for beach sports, picnics, swimming and surfing with the children and, no doubt before very long, our growing grandchildren.

PAINTINGS, SKETCHES AND DIARIES

CREDITON

Summer Evening, Crediton
Pastel, 550x750mm

CLEARLY A TOWN

*When we say it is a town we mean
it is not a bigger place grown
down; not a village getting fat
with middle age; not a shrinking
city thinned by urban anorexia.*

*A town, then,
born at four
o'clock each
morning when
milk drops onto
doorsteps along
the truant length
of Dean Street.*

*Old men stir in the night's
half-death of dawn, hear
the catch, the chink
of a soft-milkman's hard-
bottling onto tiles,
scattering cats.*

Poppies (Our Garden)
Pastel, 1016x1016mm

Friday, December 31ˢᵗ 1999

Not such a good end of the
year/millennium for Anne - down
with the 'flu'! Due to go to Evan
& Shrubbies this evening for
dinner with the 'gang'.
Shopping in the morning,
then some work in the studio
before preparing - with Anne's
help/directions our
contribution towards
the evening's festivities!
Pepper & garlic compote +
banoffee pie (Anne completed
earlier) plus a few odds &
ends!
Prepared a light meal for Anne
and then joined the others
for the dinner, but first produced
this impression of the last sunset of this century - we drank a toast to Anne, and then, well fortified we
from the bedroom window! Great meal, and company - from church, and square - to Newcombes park - thousand
joined the towns torchlit procession - twin pronged Stalls, music and spectacular fireworks. - memory sketch
there - a wonderful turnout! - a credit to Crediton! Joined Anne who is
later! Rest of party adjourned to Sims house whilst I returned home walking part way with Robin & Sue. feeling a little better!

Sunset from Studio. Diary, 31 December 1999   Watercolour, 200x200mm x 2

1ˢᵗ January - Saturday
2000

Memory sketch of fireworks
at Newcombe's last night!
Sketch of first sunrise to "match"
sunset watercolour sketch I produced
yesterday evening - good start to
the day/year/new millennium!
Anne in bed but thankfully
improving.
Cleaned thro' kitchen & living
areas - windows & furniture etc.
Car cleaned apres lunch - practical
start to the year! Walked to
park to view "after the night
before" scenario - study overlooking
church. Anne now up and
feeling a lot better but still shaky!
Prepared notes for the paintings
to be included in W.H. Patterson's
catalogue. A fairly busy start to the year, but
not too hectic. As soon as Anne is 100% we will make up for missing out on last nights celebrations!

perhaps
an evening
below - Di
& Bills. by
An
ee

Crediton Celebrations. Diary, 1 January 2000   Watercolour, 200x200mm x 2

View from House/Studio Balcony.   Diary, 2 January 2000   Watercolour, 200x200mm x 2

Winter Landscape (Redlands)
Pastel, 250x325mm

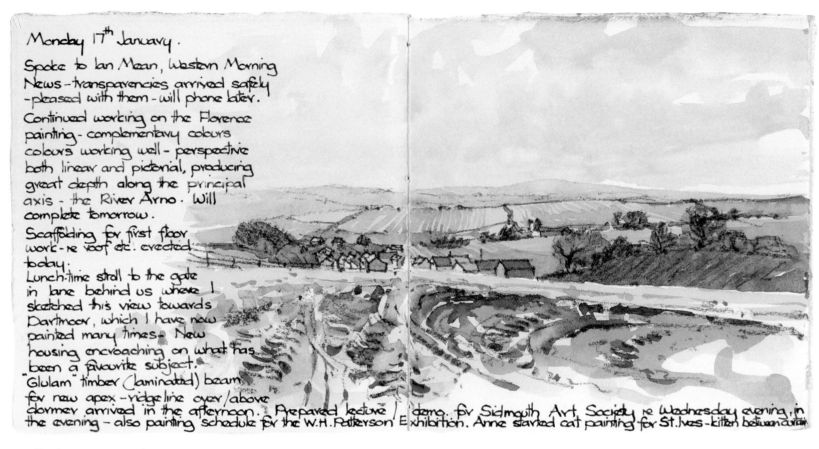

'Redlands'. Diary, Monday 17 January
Watercolour, 200x200mm x 2

The sensational start to the new millennium will be forever firmly etched upon our memories, for two principal reasons. Firstly, and sadly, it was to be the last New Year celebration to be shared in the company of dear Shrubbie, a true character of Kirton who passed away later in the year following a courageous and hard-fought battle against illness. The magnificent parish church was full for his service. The other was for the natural, outward expression of communal friendship demonstrated at Newcombes by Crediton at large, a manifestation of that special quality which is here always.

The Green
Watercolour, 180x260mm

The Green
Watercolour, 230x310mm

Saturday 1st April.

The first Saturday of
the month the day
of the Farmers Market
here in Crediton - enjoyable
walk down. Superb
fare - we purchased a loin
of pork, shoulder of
lamb, bread, sausages,
and vegetables - all naturally
and organically produced!
Wonderful social occasion
much chatter - no good
if you are in a hurry -
just so many people
to chat to - a
conversation every
few yards - and in the
High St. too!
To Guy at Trebains
for some cured ham
and salami for lunch. Kate, Trevor, Lily
and Theo (their dog) arrived at 11:30 am on
their way back from Cornwall to their home in Warwick
approx. Continued with the Gulval painting in the afternoon.
of York" behind me before superb curry prepared by Anne

Quick lunch before they continued on their way at 1:00 pm
Then this sketch of the "Green" before a pint in the Duke
then our feet up in front of telly for a relaxing evening . . .

The Green. Diary, Saturday 1 April   Watercolour, 200x200mm x 2

The Green
Watercolour, 405x305mm

People's Park
Watercolour, 305x406mm

Tuesday
7th March.
St. Boniface
Peoples Park
Crediton.
Completed painting
of Gigondas, then
down to
town for haircut,
load off my head!
This sketch produced
in Peoples Park on
return journey.
Typical red
brick & tile &
render - narrow lane
opening out & running
along at base of
open space. Important
park along south
facing hillside - we
live at the top, well
above bank of trees.
Started 'Sunflowers & Lavender Below
Mt. Ventoux' - commission - John Davies Gallery. Evening watched Man. Utd v Bordeaux away - won 2-1!. Relaxing end t'day

St Boniface, People's Park. Diary, Tuesday 7 March
Watercolour, 200x200mm x 2

Crediton. Saturday Farmers' Market (BBC's Down to Earth *– on location)*
Watercolour, 254x355mm

There is added interest to the lively Saturday (first of each month) Market when the cast of the BBC's *Down to Earth* series assembles for a filming session. It is a pity the markets are not held every Saturday. Perhaps they will, when the Fire Station is demolished and relocated, to make way for the new 'Square'. I am sure trade in the town will increase as a result, with even more people coming in to shop. This particular morning friends of ours dropped by the mock vegetable stall, and attempted to purchase some fine-looking beans. The BBC kindly gave them a bagful free! One couldn't help but wonder why one of the very excellent and genuine stalls were not used?

Saturday 18th March

Morning shopping & social chats in the town. Bought place for evening cooking session plus wine. Produced this sketch looking down North Street with our excellent Crediton Tandori Indian restaurant on the left!
Hike back up George Hill to the studio where I resumed work on Savoillan. Watched rugby on TV later in the afternoon - Italy v England. Good game - Italy did rather well although England eventually ran out winners 59-12. Completed Savoillan - Provençal lavender study - then back down the hill for a pint at the Duke of York. Then home to cook the meal - fish/plaice quite quick of course! Quiet evening there after - feet up in front of telly with Anne who had spent the day partly gardening & working on paintings for S.O.F.A.

North Street. Diary, Saturday 18 March
Watercolour, 200x200mm x 2

Study in Green. The 15th, Downes Crediton Golf Course
Pastel, 250x325mm

Studio Garden, Poppies
Pastel, 550x750mm

The Bristow's Paddock (Behind Studio).
Diary, Tuesday 11 July
Watercolour, 200x200mm x 2

In Celebration of Shrubbie. Diary, Sunday 6 August   Watercolour, 200x200mm x 2

North Street
Watercolour, 260x180mm

Parliament Street. Diary, Friday 31 March　　　　　　　　　　　　　　　　　Watercolour, 200x200mm x 2

Mid Winter, Crediton
Pastel, 325x445mm

MID DEVON

Red Fields, Redlands
Pastel, 250x325mm

Last of the Sun, Redlands
Pastel, 250x325mm

These landscapes epitomise the Mid Devon countryside, and although these views toward West Devon and Dartmoor from Redlands and Goatlake glance away from the area, the undulating folding contours, stamped with the intricate pattern of hedged fields, are the same as those portrayed later in this section, spreading out deep from the heart to the north and east of the county.

Goatlake Sunset
Pastel, 500x650mm

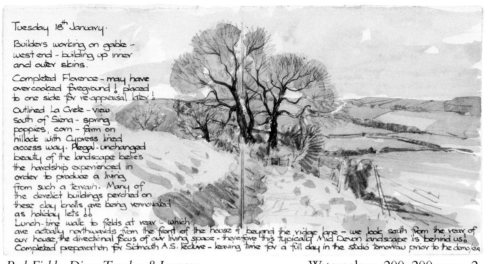

Tuesday 18th January.

Builders working on gable –
west end – building up inner
and outer skins.

Completed Florence – may have
overcooked foreground! placed
to one side for re-appraisal later!

Outlined La Crete – view
south of Siena – spring
poppies, corn – farm on
hillock with Cypress lined
access way. Regal – unchanged
beauty of the landscape belies
the hardship experienced in
order to produce a living
from such a terrain. Many of
the derelict buildings perched on
these clay knolls are being renovated
as holiday lets!!
Lunch-time walk to fields at rear – which
are actually northwards from the front of the house & beyond the ridge lane – we look south from the rear of
our house, the directional focus of our living space – therefore this typically Mid Devon landscape is behind us!
Completed preparation for Sidmouth A.S. lecture – leaving time for a full day in the studio tomorrow prior to the demo, etc.

Red Field. Diary, Tuesday 8 January   Watercolour, 200x200mm x 2

Winter Coats (Towards Creedy)   Pastel, 250x325mm

Red Field
Pastel, 400x500mm

Sandford
Watercolour, 255x204mm

Upton Hellions
Pastel, 250x325mm

Triple Red
Pastel, 250x325mm

Evening Light
Pastel, 250x325mm

Devon Red
Pastel, 250x325mm

Towards Colebrooke
Pastel, 400x500mm

Spring Prelude, Stockleigh English
Pastel, 325x250mm

Harbingers of Spring, Sandford
Pastel, 325x250mm

Chenson Woods
Pastel, 650x500mm

WIND IN THE NORTH

Shobrooke Park
Pastel, 500x650mm

From the North
a minikin wind,
to confuse;
breath enough
to flutter leaves
already fallen
on the grass,
not enough to
bring their aged
brown fellows
tree-clinging
yet for dear
life tumbling
to the ground
to rest, to rot;
not enough to
make twigs snap,
swirl the fish
and chippy news
of yesterday;
not enough to
kill, bring
dead things
to life; not
yet enough.

From the North
a night breeze,
not up to much;
but herald of
another wind
with more than
just a touch
of North.

Shobrooke Trees
Watercolour, 204x204mm

Autumn Glow, Shobrooke Park
Watercolour, 406x305mm

Friday 28ᵗʰ July.

Full day in the studio - Florence painting completed apart from some adjustment and final touches to the foreground. Payment received from the Walker Gallery, Honiton for small painting "Summer Gold" exhibition sales continue. Anne continued with her painting "The Daisy Chain Hat" - super work! This sketch in the top field before completing V.A.T. form ... Lily very good - trouble free baby sitting whilst Trevor & Kate out to cinema!

Mid Devon Landscape. Diary, Friday 28 July   Watercolour, 200x200mm x 2

Mid Devon Landscape. Near Cadeleigh   Pastel, 250x325mm

Mid Devon Landscape
Watercolour, 305x406mm

Devon Fields
Pastel, 250 x 325mm

Red Fields, Mid Devon
Pastel, 250 x 325mm

These views into Mid Devon from the high point of Windwhistle on the Crediton to Bickleigh road present the rural landscape at its best, red vibrant fields contrasting with verdant pastureland, spreading into the distance as far as North Devon, bathed in the clear but soft Devon light.

Windwhistle Corner
Pastel, 250x325mm

Mid Devon Sunset
Pastel, 400x500mm

Winter Folds
Pastel, 250x325mm

Devon Lane. Diary, Wednesday 5 April Watercolour, 200x200mm x 2

Bickleigh Castle Watercolour, 310x420mm

Pitt Farm and Exe Valley
Pastel, 250x325mm

Above the Exe Valley to Sidmouth Gap
Pastel, 250x325mm

Tranquility, Grand Western Canal, Sampford Peverell
Pastel, 500x650mm

Exhibited South West Academy, 2003

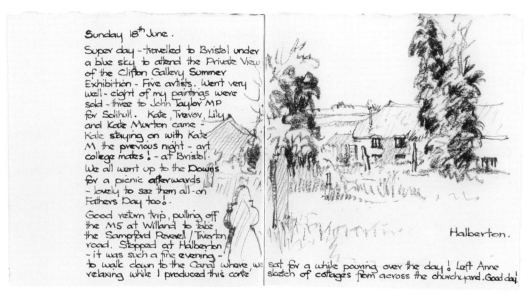

Churchyard, Halberton. Diary, Sunday 18 June   Conté, 200x200mm x 2

RURALITY

We shrugged the city off, brushed away
its urban scurf, went west to watch
the rhythm of the sun bed down to rest,
white to yellow, blood to mellow red.

The day grew grey.

Instead we watched the rain flush out
the gutter-rust, roan-streak the cheeks
of window panes. We listened with delicious
shiver to gusty winds in chimney stacks.

'The sun is dead', the people said, 'It's
buried in the churchyard near the yew.'

We stood beside the new-dug grave, saw
how the sun had cried before it died, how
tears had burned the stained grass brown;
and we recalled last year when the farmers

came to town they had had a different
moan. 'The sky is crucible,' they mourned;
'The sea is melted dry. And even earth

is turned to stone, deaf to the shout of
countryside. We will never cut our corn.
Ears stay stubbornly unripe, bone hard
of hearing, crucified upon a stalk

and nearing death, withdrawn and withered
on their cord, strangled in the act of birth,

unborn.' The people stood, shrugged,
uncertain whether suns would rise again.
Should they compromise with cold,
the cheerless weather? Should they strike

a demon deal with the cruel, the rural dark?

Winter, Posbury, Near Crediton
Pastel, 235x210mm

Winter Games, Posbury
Pastel, 210x235mm

Red Fields, Posbury
Pastel, 500x650mm

Breeze, Towards Posbury
Pastel, 500x650mm

Mid Winter, Posbury
Pastel, 500x650mm

Winter Shadows, Posbury
Pastel, 175x225mm

Long Shadows
Pastel, 250x325mm

THE MOORS

Early Spring, Teign Valley (Near Steps Bridge)
Pastel, 800x600mm

Within the sketch (handwritten):

Sunday 5th March

Cleaned Mini, then we went to Steps Bridge for a super walk up the River Teign to Stafford Bridge and back. Wonderful glades of sunlit wild daffodils – much of course than the cultivated varieties. Produced several studies and this diary sketch. A beautiful clear spring day with strong tonal contrasts to be found looking into / towards the sun. Home – then admin – chicken roast + telly-sublime

Teign Valley, Dunsford Wood. Diary, Sunday 5 March
Watercolour, 200x200mm x 2

Although the air and light on Dartmoor is extremely pure, it is, however, quite soft compared with that experienced over the equally rugged terrain of the West Penwith in Cornwall. There, the light shimmers in its crystal vibrancy, reflected as it is on all three sides from the surrounding seascape. This softness, when combined with the brooding low cloud or mist that often enshrouds the granite tors, circles, rows, cairns, walls, pounds, reaves, cists, menhirs, mines, clappers, crosses, posts, barns, houses and churches, provides subject matter where mood, and atmosphere, reaches an intensity unique to this region.

Edge of the Moor, Moretonhampstead
Pastel, 325x500mm

Sunrise Over Shapley Common
Pastel, 500x650mm

Winter, Dartmoor
Pastel, 250x650mm

Winter Air, Shapley Common
Pastel, 175x225mm

Above Grimspound
Pastel, 250x325mm

Winter washes from these hills,
fills the river, bent-elbowed
by a frantic force to leave home,
rush rude and lonely through valley
to the swell of sea, most furious
when weather is weather worst.

Here men wandered searching
gold, found the dull heaviness
of lead. Here the old came
down to die without company,
their bleached bones lying
on moss beside the stream.

That they wintered here, here
at last laid down, is hidden
by the heather; summer work
has been to turn their fragile
fragments into whitening,
shattered headstones of past.

Grimspound
Pastel, 400x500mm

Home to some ancient tribe long gone
Who in the vastness of this wilderness
Performed familiar family routines;
Cooked and slept and loved and wept.

Lived out their lives of poverty, knowing
too well the bedfellows of neglect and pain.
did they ever leave this forbidding hill
except to die, be buried by the brook below?

We will never know their names, poor
shiverers, or discover if the valley was
a kinder brother to their bones than
these chilly stones, still as sentinels.

Their wealth was their adversity, grave-
yard of their lives. Now nature works
its building skills; the tongue-and-groove
of high country slips from focus to eternity.

Headland Warren
Pastel, 250x325mm

Bonehill Down
Pastel, 550x700mm

Bonehill Rocks
Pastel, 325x500mm

Dartmoor Light, Bonehill Rocks Above Widecombe
Pastel, 500x650mm

Bonehill Rocks
Pastel, 400x500mm

The heavy-bellied cloud, a Dartmoor signature,
pregnancy close to maternity, ready to drop,
becomes a shadow of itself.

The sky is washed with purples feeding bloom
into heather lights. In the black coarse earth
reeds root green up the stem to brown.

The spongy turf of dark cosmology lengthens
to hard lines of rocks. Everywhere are stunted
walls like wrinkles in the land.

Such barriers are no match for agile sheep
despite being grown compact to thrive
on such diminished diet.

A landscape of abandoned fields, open hills
of sedge, where men once worked now only walk,
listens to baby-talk, the babble

of gurgling streams alive because another
fertile cloud gave prolific birth to drench
this hollow trench of ground

Houndtor Down and Greator Rocks
Pastel, 325x500mm

Bowerman's Nose
Pencil, 297x210mm

Belstone Cleave
Pastel, 250x325mm

Beardown Man   Pencil, 297x210mm   *Beardown Man*   Pencil, 297x210mm

Saturday 11ᵗʰ March.

Russell called at approx.
10.15 am following
his clinic/surgery
at Chiddenbrooke –
not such a
busy morning –
but arrangement
is working well

Off to hockey –
4ᵗʰ XI v Okehampton
away on their
astro turf pitch. We
lost 2-3 after being
2-0 up at half time.
Still a good show as we were playing
their 2ⁿᵈ XI ! To the White Hart, Okehampton
for refreshments, beer and a chat with our
hosts, part of the enjoyment of any sport,
and the Hornets, or E.C.V.H. (Exeter + Culm
Vale Hornets) as we are now called, following amalgamation
with Culm, have always been renowned for our social
year I joined straight from school. Great times....
produce this sketch. Will return for full painting session. Home -

quality   from the year we started in 1957 and the
then bade farewell + made my way to Okehampton Castle to
cut lawn – pint at the Duke pre Indian takeaway – cosy night with Ann.

Okehampton Castle.

Okehampton Castle. Diary, Saturday 11 March   Watercolour, 200x200mm x 2

Sunset, Great Mis Tor
Pastel, 800x600mm

Great Mis Tor
Pastel, 500x650mm

Wheal Betsy
Pastel 500x650mm

The mine clings to an edge of moor. Even
when the wheel was busy it clung by thin
thread to profitability. Exhausted of its
ore, lead and tin and flecks of gold, colours
which have fled the ground to join the sky

of tortoise-shell, this empty edifice salutes
the sun which hurries down the western hill
to close another day. This was miner haven,
hell or heaven where they say machines still
crank and groan, still crush stone to wash,

to flow a flood of heady blood-red iron tea,
unlikely harvest, unlikely fruit. Destitute
of Devon, working-house worn out by time,
vacuum-sucked of slurry-sludge, defiant,
begotten than to set still in its wilderness.

Below Cox Tor Watercolour, 178x254mm

Hut Circle Pastel, 250x325mm

Shovel Down
Pastel, 400x500mm

Wallabrook Clapper Bridge
Oil, 200x250mm

Scorhill Circle
Pastel, 250x325mm

Passing Storm, Scorhill Circle
Pastel, 325x435mm

Hawkridge Common, South Exmoor
Pastel, 500x650mm

As mentioned in my introduction Exmoor has been rather 'short-changed' in this section, but in truth I have yet to 'paint it' extensively. It certainly deserves the accolade of being a thoroughly unique and beautiful place, less rugged than Dartmoor, and where the softer rocks have been eroded to form deep coombes with characteristic hog's-back cliffs tumbling seawards. We have explored the region over the years and I intend to paint the Exe Valley, which is surely one of the most beautiful in the country, from source to sea.

The Devon/Somerset border is conveniently kinked to take in Countisbury, Foreland Point, Lynton, Lynmouth and the Valley of the Rocks, where the moor dives in to the sea in glorious splendour. There are breathtaking views from Hollerday Hill, where peace and solace from everyday stresses can be found. The vista down the coast and across to Wales on a clear crisp frosty morning, or at sunset is unrivalled, anywhere!

Valley of the Rocks, Lynton
Watercolour, 305x406mm

EXETER AREA

Reflections, St Michael All Angels
Pastel, 325x250 mm

Although this particular view has remained unchanged for many years, the riverside has been successfully opened up to the public from the Flower Pot and St David's right down to Turf. It was a privilege to have been involved with the conservation study and design of the quayside and river frontage, where I used to fish in the fifties, and where my brother wore his hands red-raw helping with the hand-line-powered (still in use) Ferry in the mid-forties.

Bartholomew Terrace   Watercolour 178x254mm

Hoopern Fields. Diary, Monday 3 January   Watercolour 200x200mm x 2

Spring Carpet, Southernhay   Pastel, 175x225mm

Southernhay West. Diary, Wednesday 15 March   Watercolour, 200x200 mm x 2

Dix's Field
Pastel, 325x435mm

Ring a ring of crocuses
Sing a flower of choruses
Spring is here to waken us
King of seasons, plus plus

Queen follows, summertime
Greening land, warming clime
Clean the scent of wild thyme
Scene of harmony and rhyme

Fall, stern harbinger of death
Pall of mist and mellow breath
Call of migrant birds to south
Haul against the coming dearth

Mid-winter when the earth is still
Hidden nuts in nests will fill
Ride out the freeze of new-year chill
Bid in the spring and ban all ill

Spring Sentinels
Pastel, 175x200mm

Not far from Southernhay, and reached through Barnfield down to the inner bypass, daffodils provide a spring welcome to the tide of motorists coming in to the city.

Spring Shadows
Pastel, 435x325mm

A family tree;
a touch chilly
for sitting spaced,
hence the hat.
It's important
to know before
we go further
which man goes
with the lady.

The tree of knowledge.

And contrary
to expectations,
it is the one who
feigns least interest;
not feigns, for indeed,
he is not interested
or impressed though
clean shaven and
well-dressed.

The tree of life.

The connected man
turns his back on the
bench tryst trying
to get going at the
other end, ignores
both friend and friend,
is alerted to who is
mounting the superior
car, parked out of mind.

The tree of good and evil.

Early Spring
Watercolour, 355x254mm

Southernhay East
Watercolour, 254x355mm

High Summer, Southernhay East
Pastel, 400x500mm

Golden Light
Pastel, 500x400mm

Morning Light
Pastel, 235x215mm

The Southernhay Plane
Pastel, 435x325mm

Self portrait.
Arms spaghettied
in an energy of sinews,
head and hoary beard change colour

in autumn
glory. Yes,
I have to tell,
the trunk is in fact an artist

trying
to look
at ease, standing
near his country residence.

This artist
thought it a pity
cars bumper to bumper,
suggests you might pretend

they are
carriages
pulled up in a private
drive; forget there is a ditch

and then
a busy road.
The trunk feels comfortable,
rooted, secure enough to be viewed

from every
angle. Come night,
the house, the artist,
his tree, retreat into anonymous solitude.

Shaft of Gold
Pastel, 235x215mm

Southernhay East
Pastel, 500x650mm

Homeward Bound
Watercolour, 260x190mm

Winter's Warmth
Pastel, 400x500 mm

Joy in Winter's Shadow
Pastel, 325x435mm

Home to a Warm Fire
Pastel, 500x675mm

Exeter School Hockey
Pastel, 250x325mm

Presentation of New Colours to the 4th Battalion The Devonshire and Dorset Regiment (The 1st Rifle Volunteers) by the Colonel-in-Chief His Royal Highness The Duke of Kent KG, GCMG, GCVO, ADC
Watercolour, 580x780mm

Summer Gold (Telegraph Hill)
Pastel, 250x325mm

Kenn
Pastel, 250x325mm

Summer Gold, Knowle Hill   Pastel, 250x325mm

'Devon Red'. Diary, Tuesday 1 August   Watercolour, 200x200mm x 2

Sunrise Over Exeter, and Exe Estuary (from Whitestone)
Pastel, 400x500mm

Off The Strand, Topsham
Watercolour, 360x260mm

Slipway, The Strand, Topsham
Watercolour, 260x180mm

Sandygate '73   Pencil, 225x300mm

Sandygate '73   Pencil, 225x300mm

Sandpit '73　　　　　　　　　Pencil, 225x300mm

Sandygate '73 (White Cottage)　　　　Pencil, 225x300mm

M5 Workings, Sandygate　　　　　Acrylic, 250x325mm

BEYOND THE HEART

The Teign Estuary
Pastel, 250x325mm

The Teign which together with the Exe has played such a part in my everyday experience, springs from the moor behind, where life, for me, began, and where the lark still sings high above Throwleigh Common.

Harvest Time Above Bishopsteignton
Pastel, 250x325mm

Torquay Lights
Pastel, 250x325mm

Sunrise, Little Haldon
Pastel, 325x500mm

Chudleigh. Diary, Saturday 25 March   Watercolour, 200x200 mm x 2

Northsands, Salcombe   Watercolour, 150x210mm
Exhibited Royal West of England Academy, 1982

The Exe Estuary from Little Haldon   Pastel, 250x325mm

Bolt Head, South Hams
Pastel, 325x250mm

Upottery and the Blackdown Hills
Watercolour, 254x355mm

Honiton
Watercolour, 305x406mm

Sidmouth Boats
Pastel, 175x225mm

Sidmouth Folk Festival. Diary, Saturday 5 August　　　Watercolour 200x200mm x 2

Impromptu Performance at the Anchor, Sidmouth Folk Festival
Pastel over acrylic wash, 400x500mm

North Devon Coast. Near Hartland Quay   Exhibited South West Academy, 2003
Pastel, 650x500mm

Clovelly, from the Hobby Drive
Pastel, 325x250mm